SCHOLASTIC
News
Nonfiction Readers

From Seed to Dandelion

by Ellen Weiss

Children's Press®
A Division of Scholastic Inc.

These content vocabulary word builders are for grades 1–2.

Subject Consultant: Emily Yates, Millennium Seed Bank Co-coordinator, Institute for Plant Biology and Conservation, Chicago Botanic Garden, Glencoe, Illinois

Reading Consultant: Cecilia Minden-Cupp, PhD, Early Literacy Consultant and Author, Chapel Hill, North Carolina

Photographs ©: cover background: jaroslava V/Shutterstock; cover left inset and throughout: Japack/age fotostock; cover center inset and throughout: Dwight R. Kuhn Photography; cover right inset: Tim Gainey/Alamy Images; back cover: Jim Cummins/The Image Bank/Getty Images; 1 and throughout: mmkarabella/Shutterstock; 4 top right: John T. Fowler; 5 top left and throughout: kzww/Shutterstock; 5 top right: Photomorgana/Corbis/Getty Images; 5 bottom right and throughout: Lynwood M. Chace/Science Source; 7: Heide Benser/Corbis/Getty Images; 8: John T. Fowler; 12: Photomorgana/Corbis/Getty Images; 13: Jim Cummins/The Image Bank/Getty Images; 16: Tim Gainey/Alamy Images; 19: David R. Frazier; 20-21: Heide Benser/Corbis/Getty Images; 23 top left: Volkan Keklik/Getty Images; 23 top right: Corbis/VCG/Getty Images; 23 bottom left: Hal Horwitz/Science Source; 23 bottom right: Ichabod/Getty Images.

Book Design: Simonsays Design!
Book Production: The Design Lab

Library of Congress Cataloging-in-Publication Data
Weiss, Ellen, 1949–
From seed to dandelion / by Ellen Weiss.
    p. cm.—(Scholastic news nonfiction readers)
Includes bibliographical references.
ISBN-13: 978-0-531-18539-1 (lib. bdg.) 978-0-531-18792-0 (pbk.)
ISBN-10: 0-531-18539-7 (lib. bdg.) 0-531-18792-6 (pbk.)
1. Dandelions—Juvenile literature. 2. Dandelions—Life cycles—
Juvenile literature. I. Title. II. Series.
QK495.C74W365 2008
583'.99—dc22   2007010066

Scholastic Inc., 557 Broadway, New York, NY 10012.

CONTENTS

WORD HUNT

Look for these words as you read. They will be in **bold**.

floret
(**flor**-ut)

petals
(**peh**-tulz)

seed
(seed)

4

fluff
(fluhf)

shoot
(shoot)

parachutes
(**peyr**-uh-shoots)

taproot
(**tap**-root)

Flowers or Weeds?

Do you ever see dandelions in your backyard?

Adults often call them weeds.

Weeds are plants that grow where you don't want them.

You do not have to plant dandelions to have them in your yard.

Many yellow dandelions are growing in this backyard.

Dandelion flowers have many yellow **petals**.

Each big, yellow flower is made of many tiny flowers.

Each tiny flower is called a **floret**.

The florets grow in tight bunches.

floret

petals

This dandelion is made up of about 150 to 200 florets.

Each tiny dandelion floret produces a **seed**.

The yellow flower petals fall off the plant. The petals are replaced by stems with white **fluff** on them.

The seeds are attached to these fluffy stems.

seed

Now this dandelion looks like a ball of fluff.

Dandelion fluff is perfect for traveling on the air.

Each bit of fluff carries one seed. The seeds ride the wind like tiny **parachutes**.

Soon, the dandelion seeds drop to the ground.

parachute

Did you ever blow the fluff off of a dandelion?

Water in the ground softens the seeds.

Each seed starts to grow.

First, each tiny seed sends out a **taproot**.

A taproot is a long, strong root. It grows straight down into the ground.

Smaller roots grow from the taproot as the plant gets bigger.

taproot

Smaller roots branch out from a dandelion's taproot.

Then a green **shoot** pokes out above the ground.

The plant grows bigger. It grows leaves and a flower.

Soon a new dandelion flower will bloom.

bloom

This shoot is growing from a seed that is still attached to its bit of fluff.

Did you ever try to pull a dandelion out of the ground?

If you don't dig out the whole taproot, a new plant will grow.

All those seeds and those strong taproots mean one thing.

It is hard to keep dandelions out of your backyard!

DANDELION LIFE CYCLE

1

A dandelion seed floats on the air. Then it lands on the soil.

2

The seed starts to grow. It sends a taproot down into the soil.

5

The petals
fall off and
are replaced
by fluff.

4

A dandelion
flower blooms.

3

Soon a dandelion sprout
appears. The sprout
grows and grows.

21

YOUR NEW WORDS

floret (**flor**-ut) a small flower

fluff (fluhf) a light, soft, airy substance

parachutes (**peyr**-uh-shoots) big pieces of cloth used to help people or objects fall slowly to the ground

petals (**peh**-tulz) the colored outer parts of flowers

seed (seed) the part of a flowering plant from which a new plant can grow

shoot (shoot) a young plant that has just appeared above the soil

taproot (**tap**-root) a long, strong root that grows straight down into the ground

MORE PLANTS WITH PARACHUTE SEEDS

asters
(**as**-turz)

cattails
(**kat**-taylz)

milkweeds
(**milk**-weedz)

thistles
(**thi**-sulz)

23

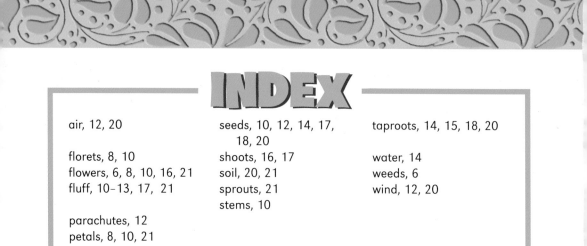

INDEX

FIND OUT MORE

Book:
Posada, Mia. *Dandelions: Stars in the Grass.* Minneapolis: Carolrhoda Books, 2000.

Website:
Celebrating Wildflowers
http://www.fs.fed.us/r6/uma/urban/taof1f.htm

MEET THE AUTHOR

Ellen Weiss has received many awards for her books for kids. She has a garden, where she is especially good at growing weeds.